W9-AMN-772

Ladders

Wild Animals

World Book

in association with

TWOCAN

World Book, Inc.
233 N. Michigan Ave.
Chicago, IL 60601
in association with Two-Can Publishing.

For information about other World Book publications, visit our
Web site http://www.worldbook.com or call 1-800-WORLDBK
(967-5325). For information about sales to schools and libraries,
call 1-800-975-3250 (United States); 1-800-837-5365 (Canada).

Written and edited by: Sarah Fecher and Deborah Kespert
Story by: Belinda Webster
Consultants: Dr. Iram Siraj-Blatchford, Institute of Education, London; Sandi Bain, London Zoo
Art director: Belinda Webster
Design: Amanda McCourt
Main illustrations: Peter Utton
Computer illustrations: Jon Stuart
U.S. Editor: Sharon Nowakowski, World Book Publishing

2006 Printing
© Two-Can Publishing, 1998

Library of Congress Cataloging-in-Publication Data
Fecher, Sarah.
    Wild animals / [written and edited by Sarah Fecher and Deborah
Kespert; story by Belinda Webster].
      p.   cm. -- (Ladders)
    Includes index.
    Summary: Introduces wild animals that live on the grasslands of
Africa, including the rhinoceros, lion, and cheetah. Features an
animal puzzle, quiz, and fictional story about the weaverbird.
      ISBN 0-7166-7707-5 (hc)   0-7166-7708-3 (sc)
      1. Animals--Miscellanea--Juvenile literature. [1. Animals.
2. Zoology--Africa.] I. Kespert, Deborah.   II. Webster, Belinda.
III. Title. IV. Series
QL49.F4125   1998
590--dc21   97-42063

Photographic credits: p4: Zefa; p6: Ardea Ltd; p7: Tony Stone Images; p8: Ardea Ltd; p10: Ardea Ltd;
p11: Tony Stone Images; p12: Tony Stone Images; p13: Planet Earth Pictures; p16: Oxford Scientific Films;
p19: Planet Earth Pictures; p20: BBC Natural History Unit; p22: BBC Natural History Unit;
p23: Natural History Photographic Agency.

Printed in China

7 8 9 10 09 08 07 06

What's inside?

In this book, you can find out about lots of exciting wild animals. All of the animals in this book live in Africa. They make their homes on dry, grassy land that stretches as far as your eyes can see.

Rhinoceros

A rhinoceros, or rhino for short, lives by itself. It spends the day dozing on the grass, nibbling at plants, and rolling around in wet mud to cool down. All the other animals keep out of its way because it looks so fierce!

A rhino pulls twigs from a bush with its long top lip. It chews the twigs with its flat, back teeth.

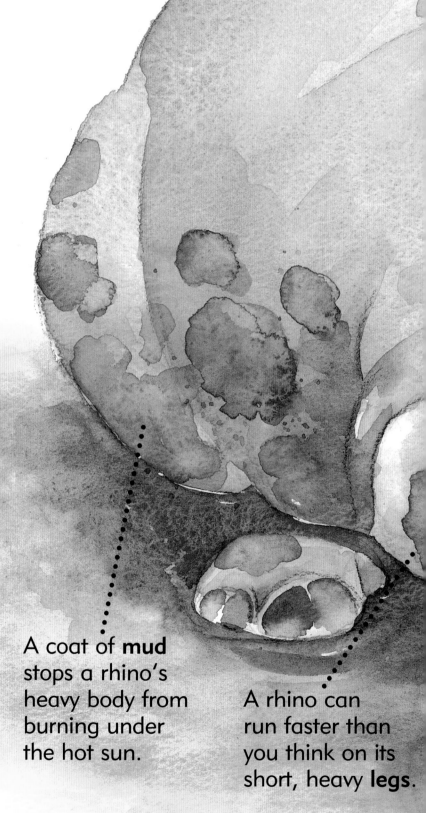

A coat of **mud** stops a rhino's heavy body from burning under the hot sun.

A rhino can run faster than you think on its short, heavy **legs**.

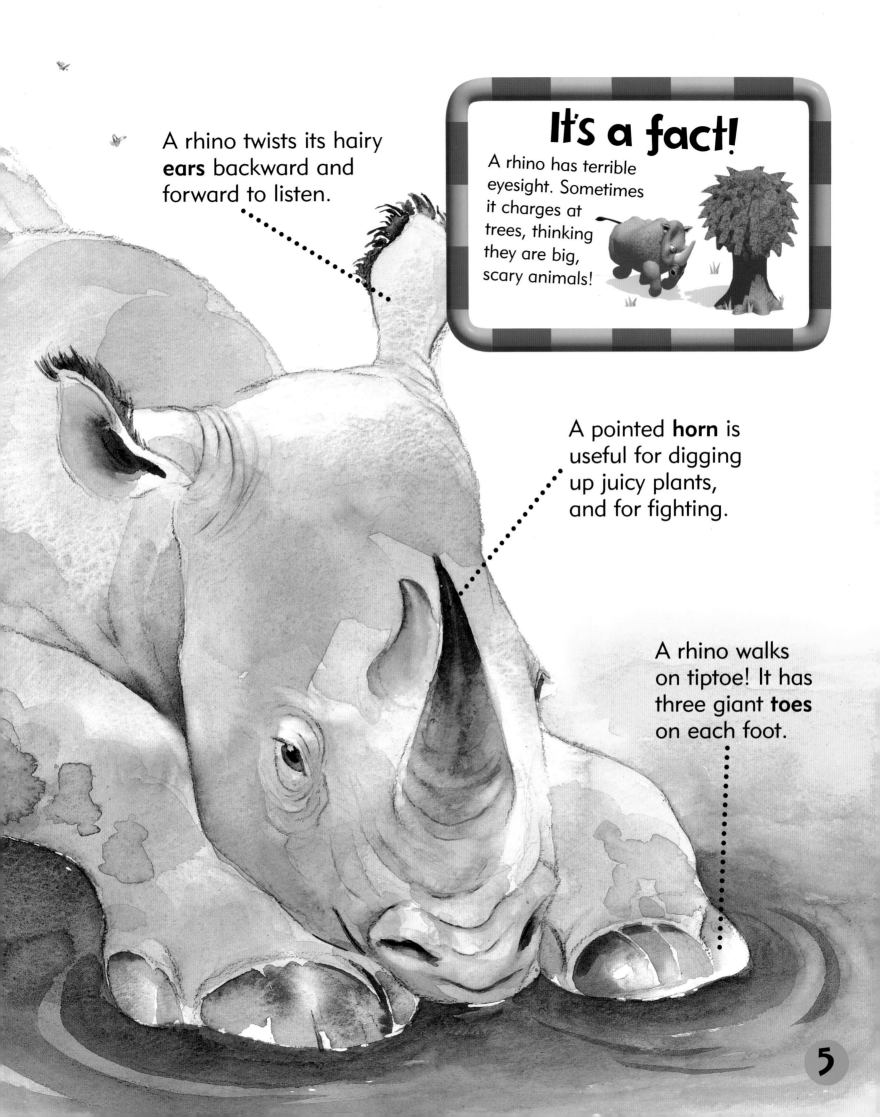

A rhino twists its hairy **ears** backward and forward to listen.

It's a fact!

A rhino has terrible eyesight. Sometimes it charges at trees, thinking they are big, scary animals!

A pointed **horn** is useful for digging up juicy plants, and for fighting.

A rhino walks on tiptoe! It has three giant **toes** on each foot.

5

Giraffe

Small groups of giraffes run across the grasslands on their long, slender legs. They are the tallest animals in the world. Giraffes aren't afraid of many animals, but they have to keep an eye out for hungry lions.

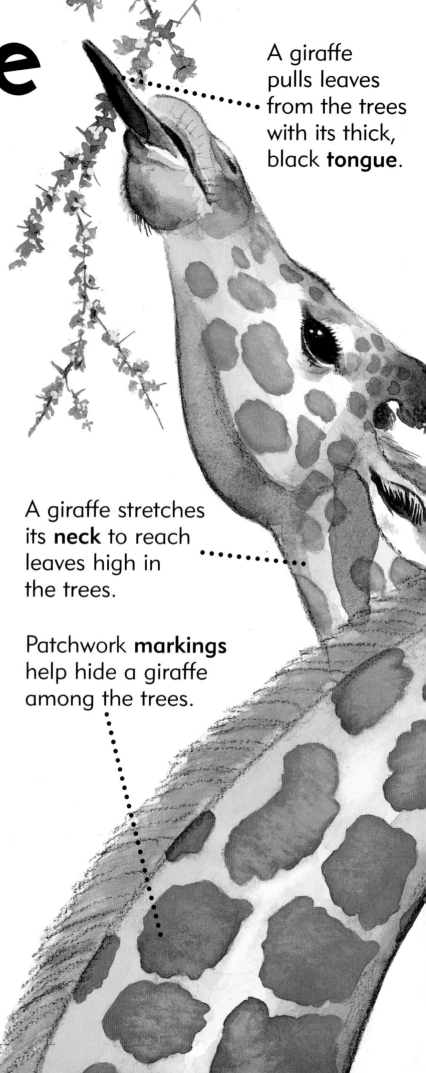

A giraffe pulls leaves from the trees with its thick, black **tongue**.

A giraffe stretches its **neck** to reach leaves high in the trees.

Patchwork **markings** help hide a giraffe among the trees.

A giraffe bends down a long way to drink. It spreads its front legs wide and carefully lowers its head.

Two bony **horns** grow from the top of a giraffe's head.

A baby giraffe takes shelter between its mother's legs. Here, it feels snug and safe from enemies.

Thick **eyelashes** protect a giraffe's eyes from wind and dust.

Even the sharpest thorns do not prick a giraffe's thick **lips** as it eats.

Hippopotamus

Hippopotamuses, or hippos for short, love to spend their days lazing around in muddy water. Here, they keep cool, away from the hot sun. At night, they climb onto the land to munch grass at the water's edge.

Wallowing in the water stops a hippo's thin **skin** from drying out.

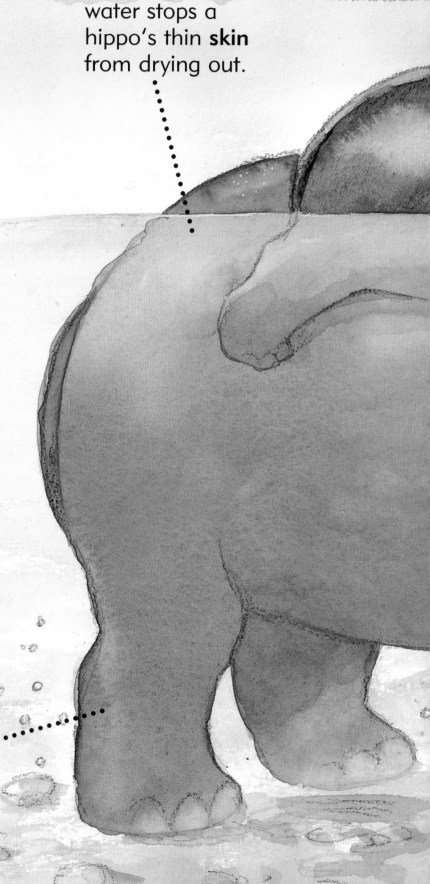

When a hippo is angry, it opens its big mouth as wide as it can and flashes its long, sharp teeth!

A hippo is an excellent swimmer, but it also enjoys **walking** along the bottom of the river.

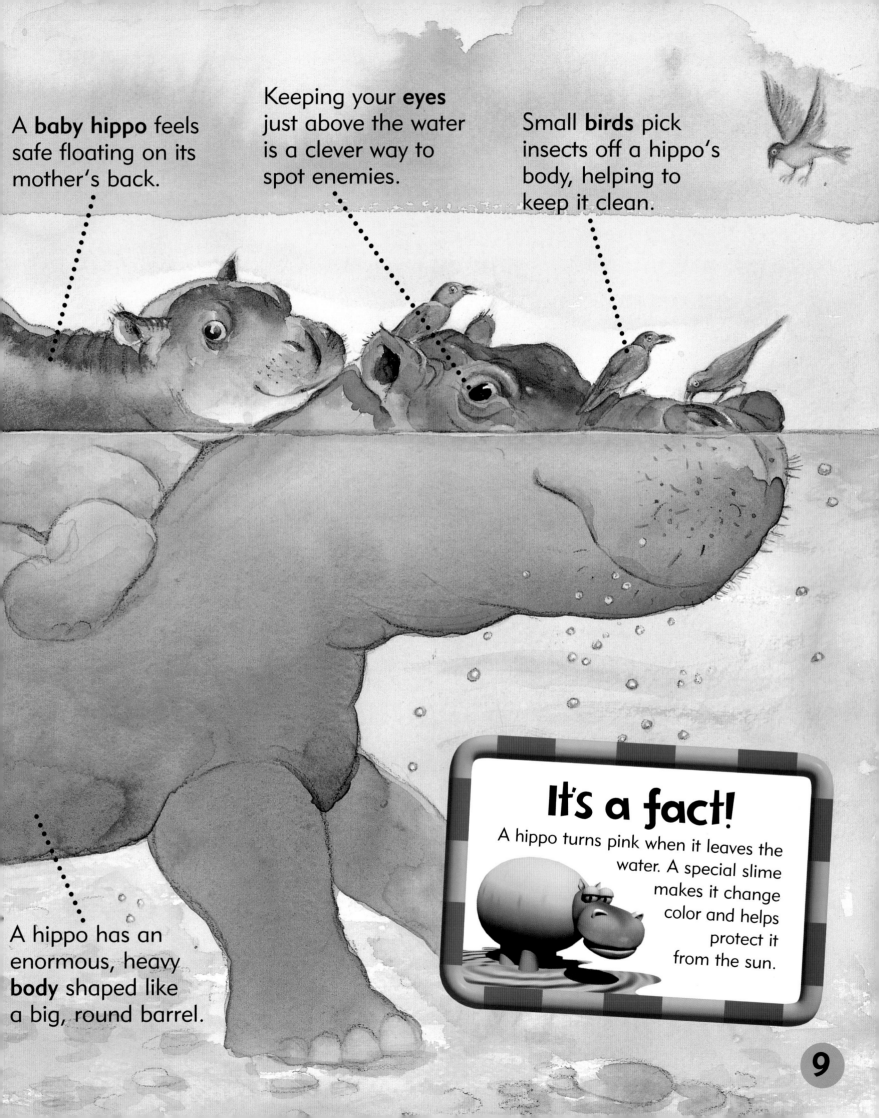

A **baby hippo** feels safe floating on its mother's back.

Keeping your **eyes** just above the water is a clever way to spot enemies.

Small **birds** pick insects off a hippo's body, helping to keep it clean.

A hippo has an enormous, heavy **body** shaped like a big, round barrel.

It's a fact!

A hippo turns pink when it leaves the water. A special slime makes it change color and helps protect it from the sun.

Zebra

Zebras are quiet animals that gather in groups. They wander around, looking for juicy grass to eat. Zebras are afraid of fierce lions. When they spot a hungry lion, they gallop off as fast as they can!

One zebra **listens** for danger while the others nibble at the grass.

A baby zebra stands up soon after it is born. At first, it wobbles on its long legs, but it quickly learns how to walk.

A zebra brushes buzzing flies away with its long **tail**.

A bony **hoof** covers each foot and protects it like a shoe.

Look closely and you'll see that the black and white **stripes** on each zebra are different!

Groups of zebras often walk for hours across the dry, hot grasslands to drink from a pool of cool water.

Thick tufts of **hair** stick up from a zebra's neck.

Big, flat **teeth** are good for chewing tough clumps of grass.

11

Lion

Powerful lions live together in groups called prides. Mother lions prowl through the grass, hunting for food. At home, a strong father lion keeps guard. When dinner arrives, the father lion always digs in first!

It's a fact!

When two lions from the same pride meet, they rub their heads together. This shows that they are friends.

A shaggy **mane** makes a father lion look big and frightening!

Thick, golden **fur** hides a lion in the dry, yellow grass.

A tired father lion finds a shady spot in a tree. He sleeps here all day long, away from the hot sun.

Sharp front **teeth** help a lion catch and grip its food.

A mighty **roar** frightens other animals away.

Baby lions are called cubs. They learn to be fierce by playing and trying to fight with the mother lions.

A lion quietly creeps up to its enemies on its soft, padded **paws**.

By the water

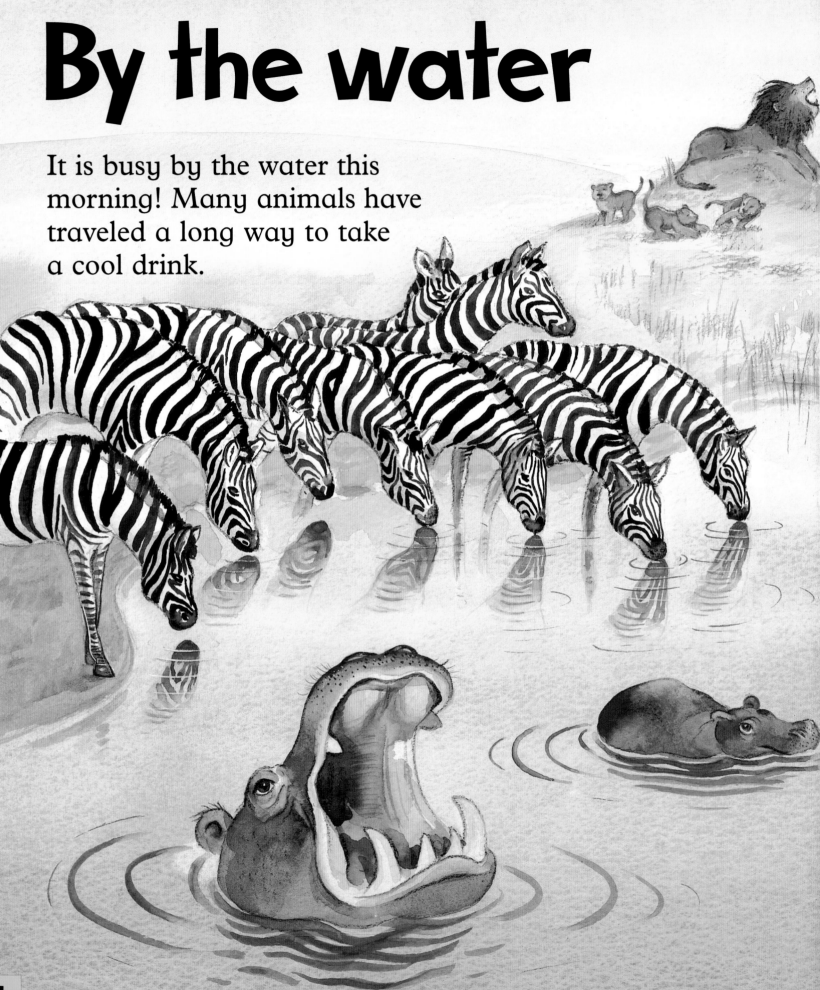

It is busy by the water this morning! Many animals have traveled a long way to take a cool drink.

What is the hungry giraffe eating?

Words you know

Here are words that you read earlier in this book. Say them out loud, then find the things in the picture.

hoof	tongue	mane
stripes	skin	horn

15

Elephant

An elephant has the longest nose in the world, but it uses its nose for more than smelling! An elephant uses its nose, called a trunk, for drinking water, carrying food, and making a loud noise just like a trumpet!

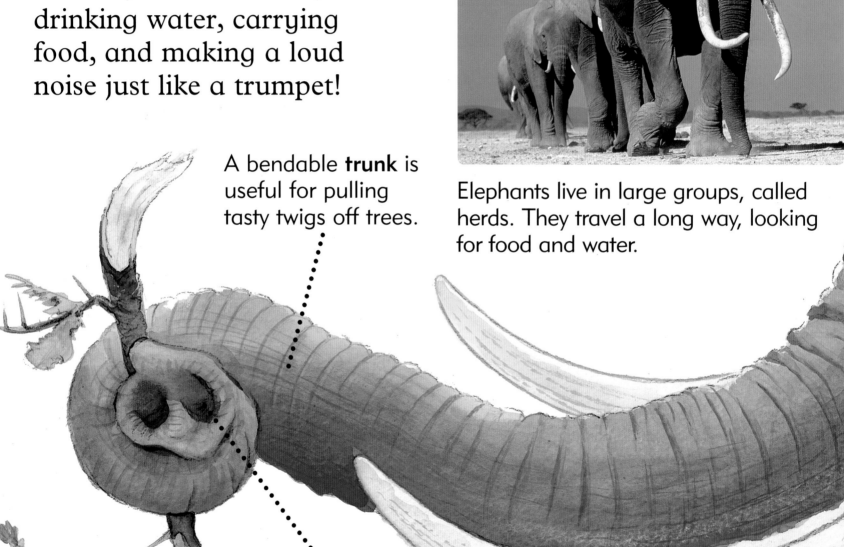

A bendable **trunk** is useful for pulling tasty twigs off trees.

Elephants live in large groups, called herds. They travel a long way, looking for food and water.

An elephant sniffs its food through two **nostrils** to find out if it is good to eat.

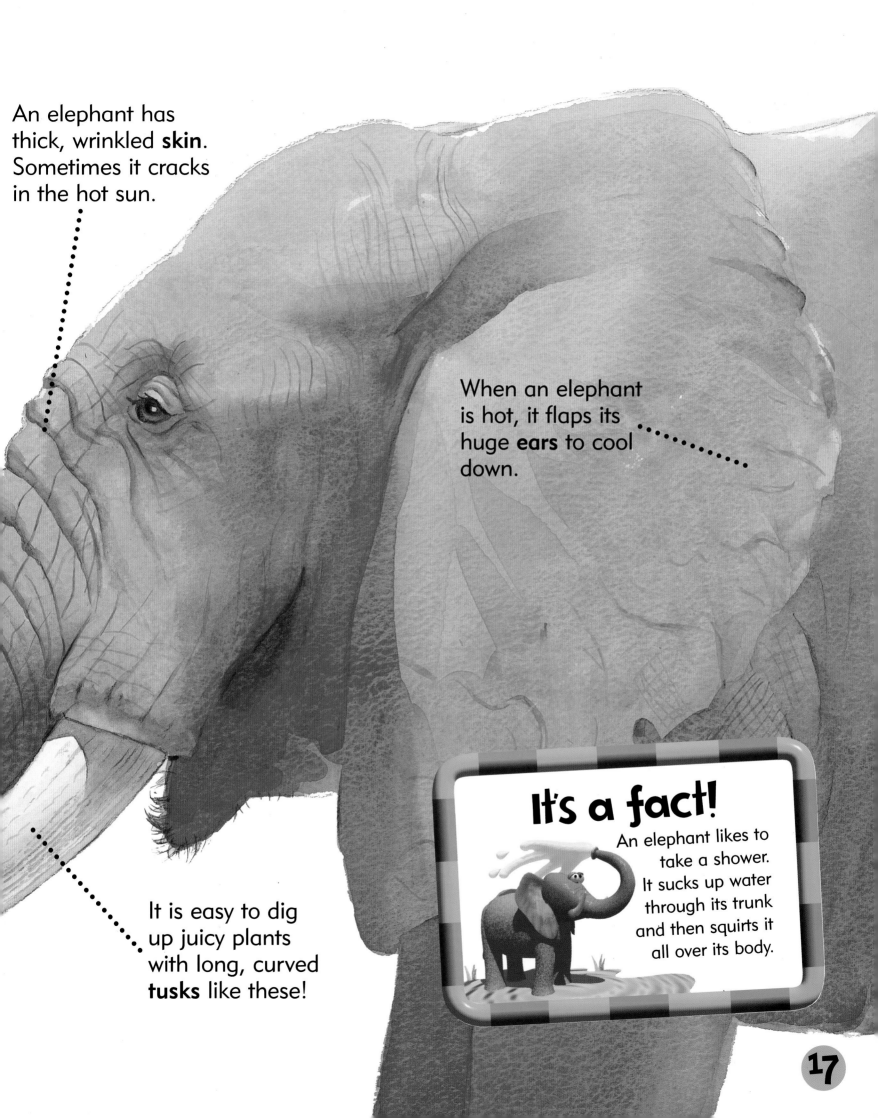

An elephant has thick, wrinkled **skin**. Sometimes it cracks in the hot sun.

When an elephant is hot, it flaps its huge **ears** to cool down.

It is easy to dig up juicy plants with long, curved **tusks** like these!

It's a fact!

An elephant likes to take a shower. It sucks up water through its trunk and then squirts it all over its body.

 # Cheetah

During the day, a sneaky cheetah hunts for its dinner. It spots an animal from far away and follows it silently through the grass. Then the cheetah leaps out and chases it as fast as it can. In seconds, the cheetah has a tasty meal!

When a cheetah turns, it holds out its **tail**. This keeps the cheetah steady.

A yellow coat with black **spots** hides a cheetah as it moves through the grass.

It's a fact!

A cheetah runs quicker than any other animal on land. Over short distances, it runs as fast as a car on a highway!

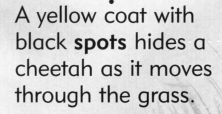

Powerful, long **legs,** such as these, are best for running quickly.

Many animals are afraid of this sharp **bite**!

Strong **claws** dig into the hard ground. Like athletic shoes with cleats, they help a cheetah run fast.

A mother cheetah looks after her silver-haired baby for many months, teaching it how to live in the wild.

# Chimpanzee

Chimpanzees, or chimps for short, live in noisy groups. They look after one another and search for food together. When they are excited, they jump up and down and scream as loud as they can.

A piggyback ride keeps a **baby chimp** safe from harm.

Young chimpanzees enjoy playing in the trees. They grip the branches tightly with their hands and feet.

A **stick** is useful for digging up ants to eat.

Keeping clean is easy. The mother picks twigs out of the baby chimp's fur.

Chimpanzees **make faces** to talk to each other. Maybe this face means "hello."

A chimpanzee walks on all fours, leaning on its **knuckles**.

It's a fact!

A chimpanzee makes its own bed! Each night, it climbs up a tree and lays down twigs and leaves where it sleeps.

Amazing birds

There are hundreds of amazing birds on the grasslands. Giant ostriches run along the ground, and tiny, colorful weaverbirds fly from tree to tree. You may even spot a hungry vulture swooping through the sky.

A vulture spots a snack from far away with a pair of beady **eyes**.

Silky **feathers** cover a vulture's body and keep it warm and dry.

A hooked **beak** is for tearing up chunks of food.

Ostriches cannot fly, but they can run very fast on their long, skinny legs.

To fly, a vulture stretches out its two huge **wings**.

A vulture can pick up tasty meals with its strong, clawed **feet**.

A weaverbird works hard to build his nest. He collects strips of grass and weaves them into a ball on a branch.

Roaming around

During the day, many wild animals are out and about. They roam across the grass looking for tasty food to eat.

24

Which noisy animals are swinging through the trees?

Words you know

Here are words that you read earlier in this book. Say them out loud, then find the things in the picture.

tusks   trunk   tail

feathers   beak   wings

Which beady-eyed bird is looking for a snack?

The most amazing weaverbird nest of all time

Weaverbird was exhausted. He'd just finished weaving the last piece of long grass into his round nest, high up in the branch of an old thorny tree.

"Wow!" thought Weaverbird. "That is the most amazing nest I have ever woven in my life. I must ask all the animals to come and look at it at once, while it is still fresh and green."

Weaverbird looked around him. Way up on the highest branch, Vulture was cleaning his wings.

"I'll invite Vulture down to have a look," he thought.

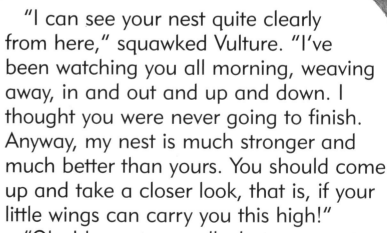

"Hey, Vulture!" he shrieked. "Hop down here and have a look at the most amazing weaverbird nest of all time."

"I can see your nest quite clearly from here," squawked Vulture. "I've been watching you all morning, weaving away, in and out and up and down. I thought you were never going to finish. Anyway, my nest is much stronger and much better than yours. You should come up and take a closer look, that is, if your little wings can carry you this high!"

"Oh, I know very well what your nest looks like," Weaverbird twittered.

Mother Rhino slowly lifted her huge, gray head and looked straight into Weaverbird's tiny eyes.

"My eyesight is not too good you know," she said, talking with her mouth full. "I'm afraid all I can see is a little green blur. It is good you told me where your nest is because I might have mistaken it for a big, fat, juicy leaf."

"Hmph," sighed Weaverbird as he did a loop-the-loop and flew off.

"It is a huge pile of old sticks, dead grass, and feathers. You don't know how to weave at all!"

But before Vulture could ruffle his feathers, Weaverbird did a loop-the-loop and flew off.

As usual, Mother Rhino and her little baby were standing nearby, munching on their favorite bush.

"Hey, Mother Rhino," Weaverbird chirped. "Stop eating for a minute, will you, and look up over your horn. I've just finished weaving the most amazing weaverbird nest of all time."

"I know what I will do," thought Weaverbird. "I will fly to the forest and ask the chimpanzees. They are awfully clever. I have seen them using sticks to dig tiny insects out of the ground. They must have good eyesight if they can see things that are so small."

When Weaverbird landed in the forest, he could hear the chimps chattering about in the trees.

"Hey, chimps!" he shouted through the leaves, "I have made the most amazing weaverbird nest of all time, and I would like you all to come and see it."

"Why should we swing all the way over there?" they hooted. "We are not interested in one of those teeny, weeny, grass ball nests that you spend all day weaving, in and out, and up and down.

We have the most comfortable nests in the entire world. We build our nests every night out of fresh leaves and twigs on any branch we like."

"Every night," laughed Weaverbird, "before you go to sleep. What a lot of work!"

But before they could make a face, Weaverbird did a loop-the-loop and flew off.

28

On his way back to the old thorny tree, Weaverbird looked down and saw Cheetah snoozing in the long grass.

"He looks like he has had a good dinner," thought Weaverbird. "Perhaps that has put him in a good mood."

Weaverbird swooped down to where Cheetah lay and hovered by his head.

"Hey, Cheetah," he whispered, "I have made the most amazing weaverbird nest of all time. Would you like to see it?"

Cheetah opened his eyes and yawned, flashing his long, sharp teeth.

"I am not scared of you," piped up Weaverbird. "Catch me if you can!"

But before Cheetah could open his mouth, Weaverbird did a loop-the-loop and flew off.

Feeling rather thirsty after all his squawking, Weaverbird decided to stop for a drink at the water hole. Just as he dipped his beak, a big herd of zebras joined him at the water's edge.

"They will know a thing or two about grass," thought Weaverbird. "They spend all day with their noses in it."

"Well knock my spots off," he hissed angrily. "You must be joking. I cannot be bothered with fiddly weavy stuff. This whole grassland is my nest. Whenever I want to relax, all I have to do is lie down in the grass or climb a tree." Cheetah stretched and then yawned. "Most of the animals keep out of my way. I usually go looking for THEM when I am hungry."

"Hey, zebras!" chirped Weaverbird. "You know all about grass. Would you like to come over and look at the most amazing weaverbird nest of all time?"

"Oh yes, we would love to," they replied enthusiastically. "All we ever do is eat and drink. It would be such fun to do something different."

"Well then, follow me!" yelled Weaverbird. The zebras quickly trotted after him to the bottom of the old thorny tree.

"So where exactly is your nest?" snorted the zebras.

"Stretch your necks and open your eyes," said Weaverbird, pointing above their heads.

"Wow!" said one zebra.

"That really is the most amazing weaverbird nest of all time," said another.

"You could not have made that all by yourself," said a third. "You must have had some help!"

"No," said Weaverbird proudly, "I made it all by myself."

"Well, well, well, well, well," said the zebras, one after the other.

"We have seen a lot of grass in our time, but we've certainly never seen anything this amazing. All that lovely green grass woven together to make a beautiful bird's nest. You must be extremely clever."

Weaverbird was thrilled. "Thank you, thank you," he said, taking a bow and hanging upside down from his nest, trying to impress the zebras with his flying acrobatics.

And with one final bow, Weaverbird did a loop-the-loop and flew off to look for a friend to share his lovely little nest.

Puzzles

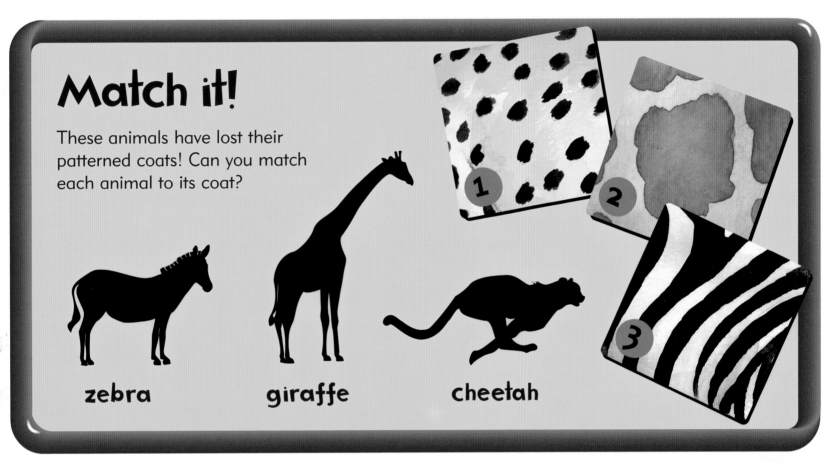

Match it!

These animals have lost their patterned coats! Can you match each animal to its coat?

zebra giraffe cheetah

1
2
3

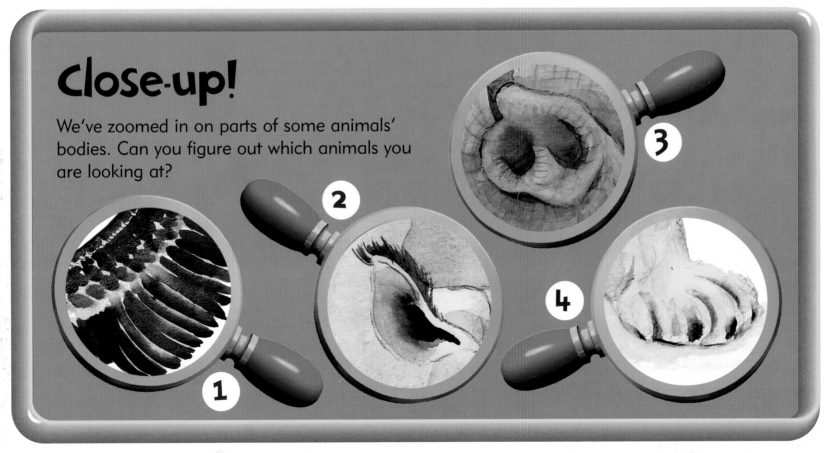

Close-up!

We've zoomed in on parts of some animals' bodies. Can you figure out which animals you are looking at?

1
2
3
4

True or false quiz

Can you figure out which animals are telling the truth? You can go to the page numbers listed to help find out the answers.

1 A cheetah can run as fast as a car. **Go to page 18.**

2 Hippos turn green when they leave the water. **Go to page 9.**

3 When two lions from the same pride meet, they rub heads to say hello. **Go to page 12.**

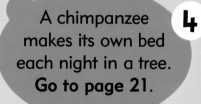

4 A chimpanzee makes its own bed each night in a tree. **Go to page 21.**

Answers: 1 true, 2 false, 3 true, 4 true.

Index